The Machinery of Grace

The Machinery of Grace

Cento Poems by

Patrice Boyer Claeys

Cover design: Samata

Cover art: *Twisting Female Torso,* by Eric Boyer
www.boyermesh.com

ISBN: 978-1-950462-73-5

Kelsay Books Inc.

kelsaybooks.com

502 S 1040 E, A119
American Fork, Utah 84003

for my mother

Ruth Basler Boyer
1928-2013

❦

Acknowledgments

My deep appreciation to the journals in which versions of these poems first appeared.

Aeolian Harp Anthology Series: "To My Sister, One Year After Placing My Mother's Ashes in the Lake," "Jazzed"

Eclectica Magazine: "Hard Energy," "As If Language Resisted Death"

Found Poetry Review: "The First Autumn Following Her Death," "Jazzed"

Highland Park Poetry: "Getting Through"

Light: A Journal of Photography and Poetry: "On Placing My Mother's Ashes in Lake Winnipesaukee"

Northwest Cultural Council Poet and Artist Chapbook: "The World Uncloses Its Round Heart" (as "Cento of Sadness")

Origami Poems Project: "In the Garbled Language of Dementia," "Like someone lost in a forest" (as "While I'm inside this darkness I can see"), "My Words Come Back," "Renewal," "Life Lesson," "In the end"

Relief: A Journal of Art and Faith: "Bedside Vigil," "The Machinery of Grace Is Always Simple"

South 85 Journal: "Of the Hand That Made Me"

Unlost Journal: "Rebirth" (as "Birth")

"The machinery of grace" is a phrase borrowed from "Machines," by Michael Donaghy.

Special thanks to my perceptive and generous readers, Gail Goepfert and Barbara Kreader Skalinder.

Contents

ॐ॰ॐ॰ॐ॰ॐ

This Life

Longing consumes us
from skull to tailbone.
And the sound of our deepest voice
rattles the long throat of the horizon.

We have
risen from roots
born to age and die. How
I wish we had
sweet words,
a helix of song
like the ring of crystal against crystal
instead of this
world always falling
no matter what you do.

Between us and the sun
is the wheel that brings it round,
and what I hear is my whole self
hard as the earth, sheer, present as the sea:

this life, this life, this life.

Hard Energy

The sea cries with its meaningless voice.
It flies through itself like light. It sails
into broken syllables of want
like a woman looking backward.

And it is large. And it grows larger—
a force determined
washing over the world.

I'm reminded of
hard energy, like the stars.

The Beginning of Forgetting

When she wakes, she feels the cold—
lips, toes and fingers like pale blue orchids,
her eyes half closed and flat gray.
It is night, dark.

A house's dark corners
become a kind of presence
with monsters hammered down.

She has nothing to be afraid of anymore.

Her childhood streets,
those old recipes she'd been saving,
now seem to her simply
a sieve, a story
of how we learn to comfort ourselves.

All this time, and it comes back like this—
the end humming along

unstoppable as water.

In the Garbled Language of Dementia

When I look inside her room,
into the unfamiliar emptiness,
a small, dark, steel coil and its detached tongue
go on and on
like song within a trinket box.

For years even my mother chose to believe
heaven had scrubbed itself blue and forgetful.
Such fiction hurts us.

        I know this:
more than once she must have heard it,
Go on, it's over,
whispering in all that wreckage.

The Drift of Your Life, the Slope

I was looking at your face, at
your intention to let go.
Forgive me
the suffering of which I wasn't aware.

And if I'm honest, of course I was jealous, though,
wished I were the one
that made your heart race faster.
You shooed me from the frame;
I'd bite my lip until it bled.

Instead of apologizing,
I'll show you how to turn to rain—
teardrops on my cheeks
and throat.

I didn't see it,
the importance of
my life,
of myself,
how I belong to you.

Do not think of it. Keep going forward
into the pocket of air,
like morning through split curtains
and gold hidden in satin.

Bedside Vigil

What I can tell you is
death also stopped,
fanned out like wings under her arms
moving between the first world and the second
into time, flame.

In order to tell you about it
I kneel beside
what power is at work, drenched there,
dew on the knuckle.
How else to encompass both the crying and those
gold wings, folded like cloth?

Before our eyes
a dreaming with open eyes
until the shell of her was blank…and yet we took
some shining thing inside us that has
the importance of beauty—
music now—
the great drum turning
and the spirit hissing away.

Like someone lost in a forest

I don't know any more than you.

While I'm inside this darkness I can see
along a giant whip,
sashes of grief whipping my back,
the threads pulled fine.

I do not care about religion
but I see it more like
the soft cold lips of belief,
like a kiss on the neck
so cold and so
hard, as so much is.

On Placing My Mother's Ashes in Lake Winnipesaukee

The sun is laying down over the grass,
over the far shore of the lake, now her habitation.

In the damp iron shadows
we watch as summer drains the sky.

If the thought of vanishing from the world
follows the deepening greens,

then I trace love's loss to the origin of light
that wavers in a match flame.

The landscape has the look of something
I have to keep.

Clouds thin into form: a hawk
touches in its sweep

the thin black seam.

My Words Come Back

I believe there is something else,
a part of ourselves always
groping blindly down a page,
saying what is true,
a language thick
with conviction
that waits, trips at the door of grace.

The Machinery of Grace Is Always Simple

A pretty girl in a wedding dress
white and effortless, hungry
to step outside of time, to grow.
And somehow in mid-air this boy is riding a ship,
forever posed as husband.
Here are his gifts: smudges of bud,
blossoms of moss.

Here is how an hour embraces an hour
and the sun is stopped still.

To love him after all, is all.

My Infant Self Gives My Mother a Gift

When she turned 19
her beautiful body ran full out,
and stallions for the night's desire
gathered themselves to blood,
a drifted, secret, bitter ecstasy.

As she shrugged childhood,
broke from the shadows,
a dull pearl—
my face—became a living touch,
and they laid me on her, breathing.

Her eyes deepened until they shone from far away,
and she said,
I was very lonely.

My own skin
talked to her, that song
of a newborn.

> *Mother,*
> *proceed boldly.*
> *You are the center.*
> *Now there are two of you.*

If My Mother Had Spoken of Her Childhood

Only child.
Not quite what one would choose.

I wanted
screaming and giggling,
  the kind I never had.

*

I survived.

*

On dying,
my mother
left me
alone with him.

  A white distance entered—
    everything ever after
   gnarled with cold, with cramp.

By *family,*
I wanted
  fertile voices—
    begging praline, pennies, scraps of red ribbons.

I wanted to make them mine.

Instead,

my feet crunching on the crushed granite
succumbed to a slow ache,
a body without
  an intimacy.

                                        I myself have missed
            my own pleasure.

I chewed up spoonfuls
of a dream remembered,
        and a loneliness creeped
            under a load of time.

*

Twenty years passed.

*

Before my very eyes
            regeneration,
                    wholeness.

It is like peering into my own body
to savor what arrives—
                    another mouth
            flat and warm as a cat.

Baths and plums,
            the plastic ballerina spinning.
        Sneakers and T-shirts playing

                                        Find me!

in a field that always fills with fireflies.

*

In my life I have done one good thing—

            given life.

The Closest I Have Come to Seeing It

Crisp air,
and homemade waffles for breakfast.
Only yesterday my mother
lifting a pot
with a warm brick of chocolate surrendering to simmered milk.

My brother is first to leave the table.
We are still new-leafed, slip-tongued,
with every step
posing further questions.

Strange to me now
after all these years I can still hear
Wake up, wake up,
taste the morning rush,

keep reaching into the past
for that muscle memory of love.

Morning Chores

It had to be done just so—
mowing
raking
clothes cleaned, ironed, mended, replaced
on the stairway.

Hey! Hey kids!
streams from her tongue.

Put to work
in the heavy heat of August.

Webs and weeds
in the battered petunias—every
activity lights
an algebra of swirling particles.

Toothpaste tubes wrung rigid and dry
in the blue bin lined with a thirteen-gallon bag.

Planning new curtains for the living room
and grunting and sweating under a shopping load.

Her milk-white clothes hang on the line
still dripping water.
Ironing hangs dejectedly over a chair
and the radio station of choice adores Perry Como's croon.

*

Mother,
I hope in the next life there's none of this stuff.

The clock moves faster than we do.
There are so many things to miss
while doing dishes.

Of the Hand That Made Me

In a dream
she's just as she was then,
and I am doing laundry, the basement windows
with matted cobwebs,
on each counter and shelf, dust
and not enough air.

In our family room
my mother laughs.
I reconstruct her—
her sorrow and pleasure equally manifest
a part of her always
rolling cookie dough into orbs
wanting to be sure
she would teach us to be the mother.

Her chewing red mouth,
which grieving does not sweeten,
twitched into a mosaic,
all broke   and scattered   and shimmered.

It's the oldest form of love—
a history encoded in our flesh which fastens us to the earth
under the stone   under the bone

where sky and ocean meet

in her silver absence.

The First Autumn Following Her Death

Of smoke-grey fog, of stone-grey field and tree
of an old cedar at the waterside
of waters in a land of change

of muskrat and shrew, disintegrated suns
of shattered moonlight and beasts and trees
of fine Spanish trees gone up in flames.

Of quiet birds in circled flight
of revelation, all the notes they'd thrown
of grief that could sound like curious elation.

Of unapplauding hands and broken song,
of her face, as open to all of us in death
of nerve and star into this evolved.

Of ripened memory which is twice
of light, a grainstorm
of something more permanent.

Of the news of this world where the air
of our bodies
of ourselves, the talking engines of our day

of bookstores and stationery shops
of Earl Grey, the two black turtlenecks
of the soon to-be-actual.

Of intertwining time and place
of a winter that no longer comes.

Getting Through

Bundled in wool,
I waited too long to drink my tea.
Here in the dead center of January, I can
stand sleeping in the cold
but could live without
the chill of sundown.

I want to be a bubble trapped in amber,
a slender wavering light like a minnow
on water spiked with flakes.

I want to believe there is enough
between me and the rock
to draw our darkest place to light.

The World Uncloses Its Round Heart

I hear the deep *pom pom pom*
and trip over roots
under a sycamore, and all things keep
the untaught harmony of spring,
leaving behind a silence.

Her shadow slips under the threshold
of a gnarled oak, stripped bare,
and has the power
to make my heart trip and slide and threaten to bruise.

Spring pricks a little. I get out the maps,
out of which hop frog spawn, dog song,
fingertips. Among the petals
of sugar flattening on the tongue, the elation.

If I'm not happy it must be my own fault.

This Is One Way to Say It

Yammering fire alarms.
The hollow wind.
My head on my pillow hurts,
and yet I continue to breathe, although
I know aloneness when I'm holding it.

After a time, the oblivion of sleep.

Last night I dreamed two people talking,
full of simple, joyful melody.

It is my song that's flown.

I must be
below the level of breath, beyond
the weep of it. But I know how
sometimes we almost manage
suffering and grief.

Just when you thought your history complete,
the peach trees blossom.

Life Lesson

Keep your hand rounded as if it held a peach,
something in its pink, the exact shade—
an answer
to memory's soft slippage.

As If Language Resisted Death

I keep looking around me
for what isn't there. Yet somewhere
the pulse of a phrase
does not vanish.

I believe in the soul, so far,
behind the foaming flesh.

Like all things, the secrets reorder the order of our language.

꧁꧂꧁꧂

Drinking It In

1

The sky splits into pink ribbons.
I awake and move,
and then, a cup of coffee.

2

From this bottle of beer—
its frothy feet a churning wave
soft spilling flesh—this gold
orbits around
in my mouth.

3

In a year my face will be tooled like my wallet—
wooden clapboard cheeks
amber occluded eye
and a shot of Kahlua.

4

My needs are simple—
order cocktails named after movie stars.
Their icy tails like bridal veils
are gauze around a wounded head.

5

I sipped my words
between forefinger and thumb,
swallowed the high
round rose of water.

Jazzed

A tablespoon of golden, boiling smoke
blows across
the tripping racket of a clock.
It's like a tap-dance
of dynamite,
the darkness ticking,
saying, *you, you, you,*
saying *yes*.

Now the ears of your ears awake and
begin a joyous barking,
begin to the roar of morning traffic.
It's nine o'clock in the morning, not an hour for music,
but the world offers itself to your imagination
like fresh mouths, and you'll actually be able to hear
the secret life of belly and bone.

Desire, desire, desire.

Plenty

Ruched in your arms
with the heat of your body
softening further those parts where flesh
holds the wonders of the universe inside its mazy folds,
I thought my body would catch fire.

I listened to my bloodstream
pick up the rhythm,
my heart beating,
the tip of your finger in slowness
rivering down my face and arms,
the dip into sweetness
by folds of velvet, by flesh and the muscle.

I was something I hadn't been before,
a world in wait, waiting to be explored, a body out there,
like glory, like light.

Silence starts where the body lays off.

When it cools, the skin's transparent
buzzes like tiny angels
behind our closed eyes,
tastes of
the sugar between.

To My Sister, One Year after Placing My Mother's Ashes in the Lake

Thank you for everything—
your laugh and eager shout, the out-stretched arms,
your hand as if by long practice finding the center,
casting off
the hardship, the desolation
of her on her way. And even outlined perfectly in white
she makes her way through the dark trees,
strides through my gaze to you.

The kitchen is the best place to sit.
Nothing fancy.
The eye rests, approving. Order obtains.
You carry on as best you can the task of being,
offering a hand, a sip of water, and something of faith.

Pines grow here, tall
in the shadow of blue ridges.
The sunlight scatters its small change.
You know that shimmer of water…?
that's one of the earth's most striking presents.
Into the waves, the wet feathers
we play,
go around the circle
slipping prayer for prayer into water.

Yes. Thank you.
Across the cool pine floors
shadow whispers the wall.
The murmuring rises and falls—
only night and the wind beating the grass.

I lie awake and weigh the heft of grace.

Renewal

It is spring and I am capable of anything.

From the confusing higgledy-piggledy,
chaos is what I see.

Thank God some things stay the same—
blue, the most grateful color,
so confusingly beautiful that it makes itself
into a new life.

A Garden Whose Fruit Is Joy

Joy spins the sun,
drops beautifully down
through the trees
in this time of fullness.

Closed together for one hour,
warm round my knees as I dig in
for one more bite of this
angel food
light. Into golden bars
and falling twigs of song,
our moment lies
just where you are,
wrapped in all my arms and thighs,
panning for light, happy to be here, dreaming.

Call It Something Good

I praise this morning,
the way it arrives and then grows
clear and faintly rosy,
and the sun says "yes"
with powdered gold.

It is hard not to have faith in this—
in the morning released from echoes,
from the blue-brown clay of night.

Because I have not thanked enough,
I'll give you this morning's
heart, the new tongue, the here-flower
and that turning sun.

My hands are for stringing
the best parts of things,
jotting down little things—
the click, the whir, the eddying forward.

The Way of Things

A beach,
      glass the sea spit up,
            a wave breaking some news to the shore.

Tea and cream and sugar
      at their table, two friends
            studded with chocolate chips.

The archaeology of a marriage,
      the equal partnership
            side by side like a windshield wiper.

White surfaces,
      shoots peaking above the winter snow
            in April's onion snow, quietly.

Two lumps of sweetness—
      the first ripe berry on the stem,
            peaches we devour, dusty skin and all.

Snapdragons!
      those yellow-eyed quiet men
            scattered by the wind.

A day like eggshell, its delicate center
      a patchwork of color,
            a thousand-piece puzzle.

These small gods, these
      painted rows of delicate gold
            a ring of suns, a landscape in a geode.

My own story
      my own mother
            a reminder that this is the one world

which is everyone, everywhere, always.

Rebirth

Long before there were words
the wind blew the leaves
like stolen kisses. And where the *scritch, scritch, scritch*
ran out and ran out, the brain shook as if stunned,
as if death were nowhere.

Slow hallucination
and brave music poured
on your fine and hidden fingers,
the single clenched fist lifted and ready
and your shoulder blades aching for want of wings.

In the end

her heart was red as anything—
that old metaphor,
that perfect word.

This, and my heart beside.

Cento Sources

"This Life:" Dariusz Sosnicki, Gail Goepfert, Jericho Brown, Tarfia Faizullah, R. T. Smith, Robin Shectman, Matthew Zapruder, Jo Stewart, Brendan Galvin, Dana Gioia, A. M. Brant, Steven Schroeder, Robert Long, Robley Wilson, Jr., Wendell Berry, Denise Levertov, Les Murray, Andrew Greig

"Hard Energy:" Ted Hughes, Michael Ryan, Courtney Hitson, Naomi Shihab Nye, Stephen Dobyns, Robin Shectman, R. T. Smith, Christopher Presfield, Thom Gunn

"The Beginning of Forgetting:" Rick Bursky, Patricia Barone, KB Ballentine, Dorsey Craft, Marion Starling Boyer, Chaim ben Avram, Saddiq Dzukogi, Kim Addonizio, Lucie Brock-Broido, Cory Hutchinson-Reuss, Kurt Brown, Louise Gluck, A. Van Jordan, Anna Leigh Knowles, Ella Flores, Michelle S. Reed

"In the Garbled Language of Dementia:" Genevieve DeGuzman, Owen McLeod, Francesca Bell, Rosanna Warren, Jacqueline Woodson, Nicole Caruso Garcia, Sarah Bates, Cory Hutchinson-Reuss, Haro Lee, Lara Egger, Miles Waggener, John Amen

"The Drift of Your Life, the Slope:" Cory Hutchinson-Reuss, Benjamin S. Grossberg, Cori A. Winrock, Bridget Lowe, James Logenbach, Mary Ardery, Geoff Anderson, Genevieve DeGuzman, Perry Janes, Marcene Gandolfo, Barbara Kreader Skalinder, Safia Jama, John Amen, n v baker, Prageeta Sharma, Nate Pritts, Primus St. John, Susan Howe, Wendy Cannella, Luis Cernuda, Francesca Bell, Cathy Carlisi, Leona Sevick

"Bedside Vigil:" Billy Collins, Gosta Agren, Dorianne Laux, Randall Jarrell, Jack Marshall, Quincy Troupe, Stephen Knight, Thom Gunn, Robert Frost, Anne Michaels, Deborah Harding, Alden Nowlan, Jaan Kaplinski, Albert Goldbarth, Robert Bly, Jorie Graham, Hayden Carruth, Carl Rokosi, Rita Dove

"Like someone lost in a forest:" Billy Collins, Joshua Diamond, Elizabeth Hazen, Matthew Dickman, Shanan Ballam, Jody Burke-Kaiser, Anonymous (Psalm 131), Robin Shectman, Eileen G'Sell, Kirk Schlueter, Denise Levertov, Laura Jensen

"On Placing My Mother's Ashes in Lake Winnipesaukee:" Jonathan Holden, Pattiann Rogers, John Sibley Williams, Hafizah Geter, Carl Dennis, R. T. Smith, Agha Shahid Ali, Albert Goldbarth, Marcia Southwick, M. Ayodele Heath, Liz Beasley, Mary Kinzie, Jorie Graham

"My Words Come Back:" Gail Goepfert, Matthew Rohrer, Lauren Goodwin Slaughter, Billy Collins, Mary Kinzie, Joshua Corey, Demetrius A. Buckley, Eileen G'Sell

"The Machinery of Grace Is Always Simple:" Michael Donaghy, Charles Simic, Denise Levertov, James Cihlar, P. C. Bowman, Carole Oles, David St. John, Donald Hall, Steve Hamilton, David Joshua Sharp, Mary Kinzie

"My Infant Self Gives My Mother a Gift:" Kristin LaTour, Athena Kildegaard, Mary Kinzie, Pattiann Rogers, Gjertrud Schnackenberg, Demetrius A. Buckley, Robert Hayden, Cory Hutchinson-Reuss, Leonore Hildebrandt, Rachel Richardson, Toi Derricotte, Khaled Mattawa, Dorothea Lasky, Jessica Morey-Collins, Saddiq Dzukogi, Wendy Cannella, Maya Angelou, Barbara Kreader Skalinder, Mina Loy, Kim Addonizio

"If My Mother Had Spoken of Her Childhood:" D. Nurske, Diane di Prima, Marcene Gandolfo, Kaitlin LaMoine Martin, Kelly R. Samuels, Eileen Myles, Lauren Myers-Hinkle, Natalie Eilbert, Jill Khoury, Jessica Morey-Collins, Cory Hutchinson-Reuss, Dylan Weir, KB Ballentine, Sawnie Morris, Steven Sanchez, Dorsey Craft, Emari Di Giorgio, T. J. McLemore, Peter Munro, Michelle S. Reed, Kristi Maxwell, Carrie Addington, Penelope Scambly Schott, Genvieve DeGuzman, Tony Hoagland, Anne Carson, John Logan, Henry Vaughan, Abdul Ali, Fanny Howe, Perry Janes, Dana Levin, Joshua Corey, Christian Wiman, Nicole Caruso Garcia,

Toi Derricotte, George Oppen, Jaime Zuckerman, Linda Rodriguez, Mina Loy

"The Closest I Have Come to Seeing It:" Jennifer Grotz, Phyllis Wax, Denise Duhamel, Xiaoly Li, Peter Munro, Karl Michael Iglesias, Rick Bursky, Roseanna Alice Boswell, Karen Holman, Leonore Hildebrandt, Tara E. Jay, Anna Leigh Knowles, Genevieve DeGuzman, Demetrius A. Buckley, James Cihlar, Haro Lee

"Morning Chores:" Lucas Howell, Jane Kenyon, Robert Wrigley, Tania Rochelle, Ada Limon, Ntozake Shange, Michael Dickman, Fanny Howe, Primus St. John, Roberta Hill, Colleen J. McElroy, Dana Levin, John Wilkinson, Ellen Bryant Voigt, William Matthews, Sally Van Doren, Mildred Plew Merryman, Edgar Albert Guest, Dorothy Collins Alyea, Cathy Song, Elisabeth Eybers, R. T. Smith, Jean Valentine, Maxine Kumin, Caki Wilkinson, Kristi Maxwell, Lois Parker Edstrom

"Of the Hand That Made Me:" Michael Gould, Marcene Gandolfo, Aviya Kushner, Will Durham, Geoff Anderson, Owen McLeod, Marion Starling Boyer, Francesca Bell, Steven Sanchez, Cory Hutchinson-Reuss, Amie Whittemore, Lauren Goodwin Slaughter, Kirk Schlueter, John Amen, Benjamin Garcia, Tara E. Jay, Jill Khoury, Xiaoly Li, Kelly R. Samuels, Wendy Cannella, Andrew Collard, KB Ballentine, Peter Munro, Penelope Scambly Schott

"The First Autumn Following Her Death:" Elizabeth Daryush, Robert Frost, Louise Bogan, Pattiann Rogers, Mary Ruefle, Matthew Dickman, Anonymous, Patricia Smith, Robert Hass,
Brendan Kennelly, David Wagoner, Albert Goldbarth, Joseph Brodsky, Rita Dove, Adrienne Rich, Esta Spalding, John Ashbery, Allison Joseph, David Wojahn, Mary Jo Salter, Thom Gunn, Carolyn Forche

"Getting Through:" Barbara Novack, Linda Gregg, James Wright, William Carlos Williams, Allison Funk, Ted Kooser, Richard Garcia, Allan Peterson, Sandy Longhorn, Patrick Carrington, Cherry Pickman, John P. Kristofco

"The World Uncloses Its Round Heart:" T. J. McLemore, Jimmy Santiago Baca, Amy Gerstler, Thomas Carew, Thomas Gray, George Seferis, Connie Deanovich, Sandy Longhorn, R. T. Smith, Camile Dungy, Donald Davie, Dean Young, Chloe Honum, Major Jackson, Lawrence Raab

"This Is One Way to Say It:" Esta Spalding, Louis MacNeice, Miroslav Holub, Gail Goepfert, Stephen Dobyns, Gjertrud Schnackenberg, Anonymous (Gilgamesh), Susan V. Meyers, Al Zolynas, Stanley Kunitz, Intiaz Dharker, Albert Goldbarth, Cynthia Neely, Julia Copus, Kay Ryan, Li Po

"Life Lesson:" Philip Dacey, Erin Belieu, Lisa Martin, Cherry Pickman

"As If Language Resisted Death:" Philippe Jaccottet, Mary Oliver, Liz Beasley, Helen Degen Cohen, Gary Soto, Charles Simic, Wendy Barker, Jessamyn Birrer

"Drinking It In:" Gail Goepfert, Lynn Fitzgerald, Lorrie Farrington, Jesse Millner, Rio Alma, Richard Garcia, Jan Bottiglieri, M. Ayodele Heath, Ross Gay, Gary Soto, William D. Hicks, Judith Valente, James Cihlar, Katha Pollitt, Benjamin S. Grossberg, Adrienne Rich, Dorothea Lasky, Chana Bloch, Jane Duran, Pablo Neruda

"Jazzed:" Gjertrud Schnackenberg, Galway Kinnell, Louise Bogan, Muriel Rukeyser, Gary Snyder, Miroslav Holub, Kapka Kassabova, e. e. cummings, James Merrill, Brendan Kennelly, Alden Nowlan, Mary Oliver, Nina Cassian, Delmore Schwartz, Stanley Kunitz

"Plenty:" Lisa Martin, Lindsay Ahl, Carl Phillips, Albert Goldbarth, Bruce Weigl, James Cihlar, Lee Upton, Alden Nowlan, Eileen G'Sell, Alexandra van de Kamp, Carol Thistlethwaite, Pattiann Rogers, Chase Twichell, Lea Graham, Natalie Diaz, Katherine Soniat, Patricia Barone, Jesse Millner, Dorianne Laux, Deborah Derrickson Kossman, Christopher Bursk

"To My Sister, One Year After Placing My Mother's Ashes in the Lake:" Maureen Morehead, Stephen Dobyns, Christopher Bursk, David Joshua Sharp, Cirilio F. Bautista, Pattiann Rogers, Dana Gioia, Mary Kinzie, Vladimir Holan, Selma Hill, Maxine Kumin, Dennis O'Driscoll, Jen McClanaghan, Robley Wilson, Jr., R. T. Smith, Charles Wright, David Wagoner, Albert Goldbarth, Anna Journey, Elizabeth Spires, David Kresh, Cory A. Winrock, Thomas Lux, Marie Gauthier, Dana Curtis, Tomas Transtromer, Alden Nowlan, Adam Houle

"Renewal:" Bianca Stone, Mitch Suskind, Louise Gluck, Victoria Kelly, Beckian Fritz Goldberg, Erin Belieu, Mary Jo Salter

"A Garden Whose Fruit Is Joy:" Anonymous (The Odes of Solomon), Cherry Vasconcellos, Martin Ryan, Virginia Bell, Lynn Fitzgerald, Michael Eddie Anderson, Robin Robertson, Jan Bottiglieri, Kate Hutchinson, Gail Goepfert, Louis MacNeice, Molly Peacock, Jo Shapcott, Helen Degen Cohen, Robin Robertson

"Call It Something Good:" Bridget Lowe, Jesse Millner, Kwame Dawes, Dorothea Lasky, Louise Gluck, Chana Bloch, Natalie Diaz, Wendy Barker, Major Jackson, Erin Belieu, Oliver de la Paz, Anne Marie Rooney, Desiree Bailey, Jody Burke-Kaiser, Billy Collins, David Wojahn

"The Way of Things:" Lauren Myers-Hinkle, Rainie Oet, Benjamin Gucciardi, Kristi Maxwell, Marcene Gandolfo, Christopher Bursk, Kirk Schlueter, Maxine Kumin, David Wagoner, Louise Gluck, Kimberly Dixon-Mays, KB Ballentine, Lucie Brock-Broido, William D. Hicks, Li-Young Lee, Campbell McGrath, Kwame Dawes, Laura Kasischke, Lisa Higgs, Kevin Young, Cammy Thomas, Jesse Millner, Dorianne Laux, Albert Goldbarth, Connie Deanovich, Cirilo F. Bautista, T. J. McLemore, Fay Dillof

"Rebirth:" Charles Simic, Denise Levertov, Galway Kinnell, John Berryman, Li-Young Lee, Elizabeth Bishop, Stanley Kunitz, Elizabeth Garrett, Carl Sandburg, Nina Cassian

"In the end:" Olena Kalytiak Davis, Dorothea Lasky, Richard Wilbur, Rita Dove, Emily Dickinson

Notes on process: In many poems the title is also a borrowed line and is included as a cento source. In a few poems I have broken a source line to better fit the flow of the cento.

About the Author

Patrice Boyer Claeys loves words and puzzles, which accounts for her fascination with the *cento,* a poetic form of assembled writing fragments. Born in Allentown, PA, schooled at the University of Pennsylvania and the University of Manchester, U.K., and rooted with family in the Midwest, Patrice graduated from the Writer's Studio of the University of Chicago and joined Plumb Line Poets of Evanston, Illinois. She published her first full-length book, *Lovely Daughter of the Shattering,* with Kelsay Books in 2019, and has read poems from this collection to many audiences, including members of National Alliance on Mental Illness. Her work has appeared in *Twisted Vine Literary Arts Journal, After Hours, Unlost Journal, SWWIM Every Day, Crack the Spine, Eclectica Magazine,* and the *Aeolian Harp Anthology Series,* among others, and is forthcoming in *Glassworks Magazine, The Passed Note, Literary Mama, Zone 3,* and *Pirene's Fountain.* A former reader for *Mom Egg Review,* she was nominated for the Pushcart Prize (2019) and Best of the Net (2014 and 2019). Patrice lives with her husband in Chicago and has two grown daughters. Find her at www.patriceboyerclaeys.com.

ৰ্কৰ্কৰ্কৰ্ক

Kelsay Books